GURL PLEASE

A REFORMED PEOPLE PLEASER GUIDE TO FINDING YOUR VOICE

Katie Hulbert

INTRODUCTION

I REMEMBER THE DAY I decided I no longer wanted to be a people pleaser… Oh wait, just kidding! That never happened. No, instead, in true people pleasing fashion, I just choked-down my emotions and eventually blew up on everyone in my life enough times that I thought 'I should probably change this'.

You see, people pleasers like myself try to make everyone happy. We do and say what we think others want to hear. Well, when one is a people pleaser with an alpha personality (like myself), it can be doubly confusing because our instincts are in constant conflict. As an alpha/ leader, I have my own ideas of what should happen in any given situation; however, being driven by the need to please, I would ultimately do the opposite. I would do the thing others wanted from me, I was so desperate to be liked I would ignore all my instincts and submit.

This is where the conflict and resentment inside eventually

came into play. Because let's face it, when you shove your feelings down... they like to come to the surface in a REALLY crap-tastic way. They come out sideways and ruin A LOT of relationships. So, in this is book I want to help and empower you, I want to give you the practical necessary steps to AVOID doing that. Ready? Let's go!

CHAPTER 1

HELLO, MY NAME IS KATIE and I am a people pleaser.

The funny thing is that no one looking-in would ever guess that I am; they might call me bold, brash, or even bossy and bitchy — God forbid — but, the truth is I spent years being plagued by a deep desire to be liked. And yes, I mean plagued (why I use that word will become abundantly clear in the end).

You see, I grew up in a pretty fucked-up environment. I was constantly told by my family and peers that everything about me was wrong and flawed in some way. I was labeled "overly sensitive," "too bossy," "too loud," "defiant," or even my favorite: "too fat." I heard it all, so I began to believe it. I believed all the BS people said (or otherwise implied), and so my inner struggle was born.

I can admit that some of what they said was true: I was loud! I

1

was even bossy, and admittedly a little "fat." But the problem didn't lie in the fact that they were right. The problem was the mountain of shame that was heaped upon me as a result of those words. My struggle was ultimately rooted in the fact that the things the world said about me, the true things, were deemed BAD. And so, I was continuously at war with myself, fighting my true nature — trying to BE something else. I was trying to shut down or quiet my true self and be...less bossy. Quieter. Thinner. Which is simply a recipe for disaster. Being something other than yourself so that you will be liked is the birthplace of co-dependence; which, let's face it, is at the heart of people pleasing.

If your self-esteem, or self-worth is in ANYWAY rooted in another's opinion of you... you, my friend, are codependent. I mean let's face it, we all want to be loved, seen, understood, and appreciated. We are social creatures who crave connection. It's in our core DNA as human beings. And, when we can't achieve it, we crave it even more. As a result, we inevitably start doing whatever we have to, in order to get it; and that my friends, is how a people pleaser is born!

I don't want to oversimplify by ignoring the fact that we are multi-layered individuals with endless dimensions to our personalities and overall personal make-up. We are shaped by our different stories and nuances; however, the cause of our people-pleaser tendencies seems to always boil-down to one thing: insecurity.

What is insecurity? Why is that important? Essentially, insecurity is an unsettled feeling in your core about who you are. It's like a nagging fear that something is inherently wrong with you. That there are some aspects of you that if you could somehow fix, change, heal, etc., then people could finally love you, like you, see you, or connect with you and your values.

So, what does that lead to? It leads to you spending your time trying to "fix" what's wrong with you. You spend all your time thinking that if you could just fix this inherent flaw, you would be at peace. That everyone would accept you. You would be seen, and loved — and maybe then, you could finally just relax and *be*. Unfortunately, while you are wrestling with this unreachable ideal, you are spending your life pretending to be a person you're not — and you've accepted that. Because being you, the real you, is flawed and wrong, so you can't let that part be seen or heard. No way, Jose! You think that validating the needs and desires of a flawed human would be a waste of time and energy and you won't let that happen. No, not ever. What you would rather do is choke-down those feelings, needs, and desires, and become what others want. To DO for others. To BE for others. Because maybe, just maybe, if you do that they will see you and you'll get that validation you've been longing for. Or, at the very least, they won't dislike you — because you dislike you enough (that fire does NOT need any more fuel, thank you very much).

But here's the kicker to *that* plan: doing those things (a.k.a. people pleasing) will never meet that need.

Never.

Ever.

Ever.

Why you ask? Because it's the performer in you, who is getting validated. The one who becomes what other people want. The chameleon. And, although the chameleon gets validated, that's all smoke and mirrors. It's not the real you, and so you never get what you are really looking for. Because the validation you receive from people pleasing are for things that aren't truly you. So, you get validated for things that don't actually matter — because who you are portraying isn't your true self — and the parts of you that crave validation are being ignored. And so, you are exhausted, burnt-out, and eventually resentful. Because no one is actually seeing YOU. So, you never feel seen. No one is connecting with YOU. So, you feel disconnected.

Now, of course, this way of being has a second benefit... one with which I am very familiar.

If no one can see the real you, they also can't reject the real you. That is the second anchor keeping this ugly thing called PP (people-pleasing) in place. You are in this position because you probably received the message somewhere along the way that you are "bad," "flawed," or "wrong" in some way. You have had your fair share of rejection, and you don't want to feel that anymore... so you hide the true parts of yourself — both protecting yourself from rejection and trying to gain approval by being/portraying someone you think is more "desirable."

Consider this: let's say you are really good at making paella. You are the best at it. You actually LOVE making it. You have some cooking talent, but you really only like cooking paella because you are amazing at it. Imagine now, that you have a friend in your life who has no desire to try your paella. In fact, they have made it clear they have no interest in it whatsoever. But, they have also told you that they love chocolate cake and they would love to try that if you ever made some. So, you give in and you make the cake. You don't really want to, but you do it anyway. You hope that they will like the cake and luckily, they do! In fact, they give you tons of praise on how great the cake is. The praise makes you feel good for a while, because they are appreciating your skills and that feels good; but, then the disappointment settles in because what you really wanted was for them to try the paella. You had hoped it would feel the same as if they had had your paella, but it doesn't. Because really none of you is in the cake. It was a chore. You did it in the hopes that they would want something more... i.e. your paella. But no luck. And so, you continue to do this with people again and again. Over and over. Until you eventually burn-out, because let's face it, you really only enjoy making paella. Everything else sucks in comparison. But no one seems to want what you love, so you continue to compromise and make them what they want, hoping that the praise will somehow be more fulfilling this time. Sorry to break it to you: it never is.

Can you relate to this story? Always portraying a version of yourself that is palatable to others? I mean, if you're making a cake you're using the same skills, right? It should be the same, right? WRONG. One is made with passion, love, and ease. The other is made from fear and lack. Fear begets fear. Lack begets lack. Love begets love. Ease begets ease. So, wherever you start from is where you end. If you do something from a position of fear, you stay in fear. If you do something from a place of ease, you stay in a place of ease.

So, what am I saying?

The key to your peace, joy, and energy is becoming okay with paella being your only dish. Making it fantastic and letting go of people and situations that only want cake. Now yes, I am trying to make light of things. No, I am not actually talking about paella or cake. I am, however, talking about how we all compromise WHO we are for the sake of fitting in, being liked and feeling connected. However, the irony is that it never works. Because, in addition to the fact that people are liking a partial version of you, you'll never know which part they actually like... the part that is a watered-down version of the real you, or the complete alter performer persona you've taken on in the hopes of approval. So now you are stuck in the cycle of dissatisfaction and half-truths.

Where everything is only partially satisfying, so you "keep on keeping on" in the hopes it'll change. It's like eating fat free cookies: they are totally unsatisfying (can I get an amen!) so you keep eating them in the hopes that they curb your craving. But as we know... they DON'T. Partially because they suck, but mostly because they are a watered down, half-assed version of what you really want. Had you eaten what you really wanted in the first place, you would have felt satisfied and probably eaten less. Doesn't that sound like a better way to go? But we don't do that. You know why? Because we are afraid we can't have what we really want AND exercise self-control. And do you know what that is? That's self-doubt.

You don't trust you. Which brings us back to the very beginning... where you doubt yourself, and that doubt becomes the place from which you make all your decisions. Because you believe you are *not* good enough, just as you are right now.

CHAPTER 2

OKAY SO WHAT THE HELL AM I supposed to do now?

Well, let me ask you this: What if what you think is wrong with you is actually what's great about you? What if you were so secure and proud of who you are, that it would no longer matter who approved of you and who didn't? What would it feel like to be able to truly give yourself a voice and genuinely stop giving a flying fuck about what others think?

Essentially: How awesome would it feel to be surrounded by the people who freaking LOVE paella? :)

Your peace, joy, fun, energy (and your life!) gets to be awesome — AND it gets to be what you want. If you take nothing else from this book, please know this:

You only have one life and it gets to be whatever you want it

9

to be.

You are the only one living this life—you, and only you, are walking in your shoes.

At the end of your life you will not regret all the things you did, you will regret the life you didn't live because you were afraid.

Be warry, however. Some people will try to sell you those sentiments within the confines of some sneaky little parameters. They say things like "Live your dreams, but make sure you're doing it with love," or some BS like that. I agree that doing things with love is better than anything done without it; however, what is implied with statements like this is NOT "make love a priority," what's implied is "do what you want as long as you don't upset anyone else." Those are the sneaky little parameters we impose on others. We don't even know we are doing it most of the time, but out of our own fear, we put limitations on others. Out of our fear of being judged, disliked, or misunderstood we perpetuate this idea that we can have the life we want... *but only to a point.*

Imagine life is a boxing ring, and you must live your life within the confines of this ring. Now imagine being so afraid of falling out of the ring, that you don't dare approach the ropes because you *might* fall out if you get too close. Instead, you live within an imaginary boundary that you've created and deemed safe (without ever touching the ACTUAL boundary). We do this in our lives all the time; the craziest part being that the ropes are designed to hold you in. They can take a hit. They were specifically designed to keep you safe. You don't need to worry about that yourself. But we decide to take-on that additional responsibility anyway. We are so afraid of falling out that we don't dare even APPROACH the boundary. Fear isn't all or nothing; if it can't keep you from engaging entirely, it will try to stop you from engaging to your full potential. It will create new boundaries where there don't need to be any, to keep you in its control. Fear is a tricky bugger: it will do whatever is necessary to hold you back.

Well I'm here to tell you what others won't:

FUCK THE PARAMETERS

Let me tell you something shocking: I am a Christian. Yeah, you read that right. The one dropping all the f-bombs is a Christian. But that's not even the kicker: what most people find shocking is that I truly believe everything I am telling you right now is actually biblical.

I know some of you just wrote me off. For those still reading... let me explain.

The church would have you believe that you must "behave" (which is code for *perform,* BTW) a certain way to be considered a Christian. Or, that one must act or do things a certain way in order for God to have your back. They may not say this openly from the pulpit, but they will say it in the very passive-aggressive shaming tone they use when they address your sins.

The funny thing is that what they preach is actually the opposite of what the bible says; in fact, it states: "it is for freedom that you have been set free. Therefore, do not be yoked again to the burden of slavery" Galations 5:1 (the term slavery is referring to the old way of living based on rules and fear, rather than freedom and love)

DON'T BELIEVE ME? READ THIS:

Romans 8:38-39

38 For I am convinced that neither death nor life, neither angels nor demons, [a] neither the present nor the future, nor any powers, 39 neither height nor depth, nor anything else in all creation, will be able to separate us from the love of God that is in Christ Jesus our Lord.

What this is saying is that there is NOTHING you can do, say, or be that would make God stop loving you. The bottom line is that He ADORES you and wants you to walk in a life of freedom rather than rules. There has to be a base understanding even in the realm of Christianity that God likes you and truly enjoys you AS YOU ARE. His goal is not to "fix you." His goal is to set you free from every hindrance and limitation to your freedom, joy, and peace. He wants to get rid of everything that doesn't let you access the fullness, beauty, and glory of who you really are. To be *who* you were deigned to be.

The Lord told me something one day that changed my life forever. In the OT, there is a verse "the joy of the lord is my strength," (Neh.9:10) it has been taught as if JOY is this external thing that somehow maybe you can access if you try hard enough in order to get through a difficult time. Well my head just about exploded one day as I was reading that verse and talking to God

and He said this to me: "What if what its saying is that you can take strength in knowing that I (God) take joy from knowing you?"

What. The. _____??? Did I just hear that right?

What if "the joy of the Lord" is the joy he gets from just being near *you*. Like when a new mom is spending time with her newborn baby, she just basks in the joy of their presence. They don't have to do anything to give her that joy. Just the mere fact of their existence brings her joy. What if that's what that verse means? Wouldn't that give you a lot of freaking strength? To know that the God of Heaven and Earth really likes you a lot. That he is so taken with you, he is smiling from ear to ear just watching you? That he is bubbling over with joy at your mere existence. Wouldn't that be pretty amazing? Would that provide a little strength and confidence in your life? Would you be more apt to walk around with pride in who you are knowing that he's looking at you like a proud papa?

We need to start understanding the truth. We need to stop being afraid of finding out what the truth actually is. It is only then that we can begin to live from it.

Have you ever wondered which parts of you could change your life dramatically for the better if you just stopped shoving it away? What parts of you does God see that makes Him smile?

GURL Please

What parts within yourself, that if you gave it a voice, might be a key to your freedom? Are you willing to find them, peel off the layers of shame and condemnation so that you can begin to see them as the gifts that they are? What if the thing you have deemed as your greatest flaw, is actually your greatest strength?

For me, it was my sensitivity. Despite the strength that I've been told I project, I am actually a pretty delicate flower. Unfortunately, in my formative years, my family would mock and belittle me for my fragility. So, I learned to swallow it down and pretend not to be sensitive or tender. Well, what I have learned over many years of poor choices, is that emotions are much like poop. If you aren't releasing it, it's probably gunking up your system and it will eventually backfire. All that shit has to go somewhere, otherwise it WILL poison you from the inside out. Emotions aren't inherently toxic, but when they are ignored, swallowed down, or judged, they ferment and will infect you (as well as everyone around you).

I thought I wasn't allowed to be the sensitive, sweet girl, so I built myself a shell. It was strong, tough, and made me untouchable. It seemed like the better way; like that was what people wanted me to be. However, I really wanted people to love me... the real me, the sensitive me. The one who no one was seeing anymore, because I was busy hiding in my protective shell.

I learned to swallow down all my emotions... good and bad. I packed them neatly in a box in the back of my mind labeled "do not fucking touch." As crafty as that was, it just didn't work long-term. What I know now is that when emotions are swallowed down like that, they work like a pot of boiling water... eventually you create enough steam and the lid will blow right off. And blow I did. I was pretending to be someone I wasn't, while actively hiding the parts of me that are REAL and that WANTED to be seen. I was fighting my own identity in some twisted effort to fit-in and be liked, and so the pressure in the pot would build until I exploded on everyone around me. And I did this, again and again and again. Continuously alienating everyone around me, sabotaging my own happiness due to the deep inner conflict I had around being my true self.

So, I ask you, what's the point of pretending if it doesn't fucking WORK? Deep down, we all know it doesn't. Instead of being "soft" I became "brash." I was getting the same amount rejection pretending to be someone I wasn't, and I was making myself miserable in the process.

CHAPTER 3

SO, I'LL ASK YOU AGAIN: WHAT part of you are you hiding that might actually be the key to your peace?

Let's take a few minutes and do a little exercise.

The first thing I want you to do is to take a least 10 minutes to write down everything that the world has said you "are" (athletic, smart, clumsy, loud, bossy, kind, mean etc...) All the things that the people in your life have convinced you that you are... the good, the bad, and the ugly.

Write it all down. I want you to think all the way back into your childhood. Some of these things might have some painful memories attached to them. Allow the emotion to surface with the memory. Don't fight it. Like I said before, emotions are like poop... what goes in must come out. Whatever it may be, let it come. Don't fight it. Write.

In the next box, I want you to find which of the words you have just written are actually TRUE.

Important note: There are things that will FEEL true, because you have believed and perpetuated them for so long, but the reality is there are NOT true. Or they *ARE* true, but because of the shame attached to the label you spend all your energy rejecting it.

GURL Please

When I did this exercise, one of my words was "bossy." People would always use that word: *bossy*. I had a lot of shame attached to it, because people were saying as if it was a fault. I spent years trying to tame it, apologize for it, and even water it down... but to no avail. In the end, all I felt was ashamed. Then when I did this exercise, I realized that YES, I AM bossy! And guess what? It's not a fault, it's a GIFT. My gift. I am clear on what I see, and say it with authority. That is called leadership. Do you have things like that in your life, that you need to accept and hone, rejecting the shame attached? Or are there things the world has said you "should" be that you are trying to embody that is not actually congruent with your true nature? If you listen to your gut, you will know the answer.

Write down the things that ARE you. The things that are TRUE. I AM.... I AM.... I AM....

What does it feel like to own what's TRUE and reject what's false? Sit with that feeling. Accept it. As you sit with that feeling, imagine what it would be like to feel this all the time. What does your mind's eye see? It can be literal or just metaphorical in its representation. What are you doing? Where are you? What does the air feel like around you? How does your body feel?

Let yourself sit with this for at least 5 minutes.

This is the state we are going for! To live in this place all the time is to live from your spirit. The place of total peace, acceptance, love, and grace. Come back to this image every day for the next week. Connect with the feelings again. Connect with the peace and ease of this image. Let yourself sit with it for 5 minutes every day. Remember it.

Things may come up when you sit with it. You may find it difficult to maintain the feelings, or the image might somehow change. If it does... DON'T JUDGE YOURSELF. Just observe. Take note of what happens. Take note of what comes up. We will address this next.

CHAPTER 4

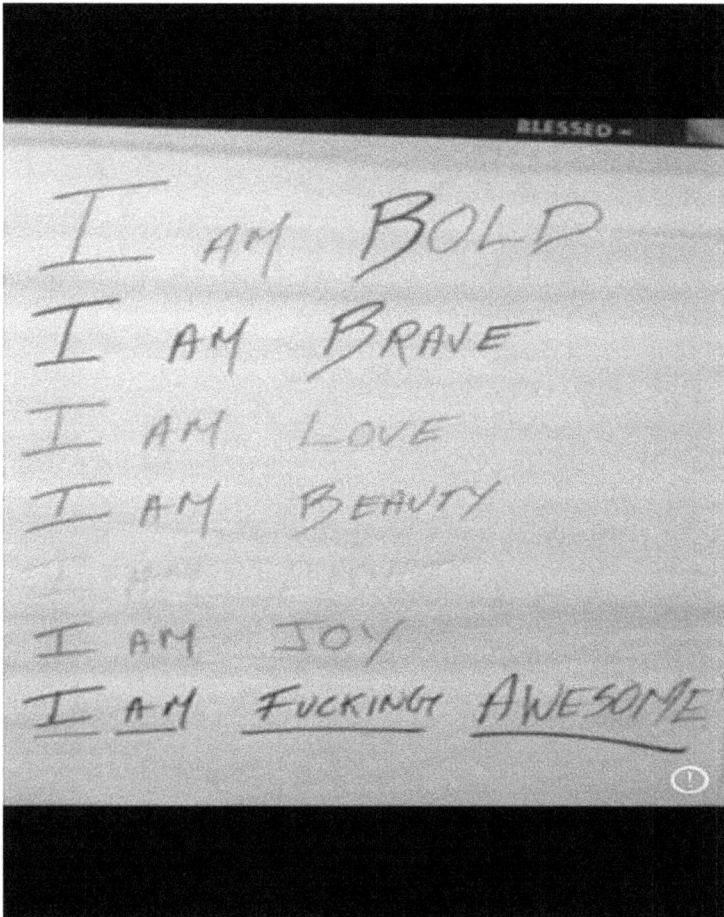

WHAT IS THIS? I CALL this my "I AM" board. There are so many voices in our modern world telling us who we should be, what to think, how to act, or what to look like. I use this as a daily a reminder of who I AM and what I choose. It's much easier and a lot more fun to stand in what you ARE, rather than to spend time resisting what you are *not*. Stop fighting to be a person you don't want to be. Stop resisiting.... it's a waste of energy. Instead, start owning who you ARE, and start allowing yourself to appear as your true self (without all the other BS attached).

So, this is the next place where the rubber meets the road: conscious choice. You can't change what you're not consciously choosing; if you are subconsciously believing or agreeing with something that is false, then that belief will run the show.

The point of the I AM board is two-fold:

To consciously choose something I WANT, and

To be HONEST with myself about what I'm subconsciously choosing.

So, what do I mean by that? I mean that when I'm being totally honest with myself, there are things that I want to own about myself (i.e. I am hot/sexy/desirable), but when I look at those things written down, I have an internal reaction that is the opposite. I look at that phrase and I think: 'But my thighs are lumpy and I have a missing tooth,' and I see all the other things that aren't perfect about me. This is called SHAME, and he's an asshole. Shame is like fear. It will try anything and everything to keep you small. So, what do I do with that?

It's not about trying to convince myself that my thighs are perfect, or that it doesn't matter that they aren't. Because they aren't perfect and no amount of pretending will change that. Instead, I redefine the word HOT. Is hot only perfection? Or is hot a woman who is confident (which I definitely am) who radiates beauty in her countenance and carries herself as such?

To me THAT is hot, so the question then becomes... am I that? To which the answer is in fact: YES!

So, my next question for you is: what are you resisting that's true about you, that if you redefined it, you could own and walk in?

Are you bold or brash? Because those words are synonymous with brave and bad-ass.

Are you quiet, meek, or shy? What if being shy and quiet was another way of saying wise and mysterious? You only speak when you think it's important. You don't showboat. You weigh your words and dole them out when paramount. You are like a ninja. Quiet but stealthy!

GURL Please

Do you see where I'm going with this? What if it's actually only a small shift in perspective that would actually free you up to embrace and enjoy yourself?

Take some time to write down the things that you WANT to claim about yourself, but have a hard time with (using this last example as a jumping off point). Go!

_____

_____

_____

_____

_____

_____

_____

_____

_____

_____

_____

_____

_____

_____

_____

So, what does this have to do with people pleasing? As I explained earlier, PP is deeply rooted in insecurity, so if you can learn to own your truth, beauty, and glory you can start to live for yourself rather than for the approval of others. Once you stop pretending, the real you can start living, being, and doing from a place of true desire, love, and confidence.

To revisit the cooking metaphor from Chapter 2: wouldn't it be awesome if you could choose to make a cake because it's what your friend likes, and you felt like it was a fun-loving gesture that you wanted to do with no expectations attached? Standing in your strength allows you the freedom of choice, which is the entire point!

People pleasing is a series of choices one makes from a place of fear, insecurity, and obligation. The way out of that is finding your true self so that you can make clean, free, conscious choices. You then can say "no, I don't want to make a cake" freely and feel no guilt or shame about it. Or, you can say "yes, I have the energy and love my friend and therefore I want to do this for them because I know it would make them feel loved."

Sometimes as a PP we want to believe we are doing a lot of things out of the kindness of our heart. But in reality, we're acting out of fear. Why you do what you do matters. It matters because obligation leads to resentment, which leads to bitterness, and this will eventually sour the relationship you once held dear. Doing nice things for someone else is wonderful, but the value of nice things lives in the conscious choice to do that thing — NOT in the thing itself. If you want to be nice, be transparent. Love is being truthful and giving willingly, not begrudgingly.

That is not to say that you should try to stop resenting doing what you are doing. But rather, I suggest you stop doing what you don't really want to do so resentment has no place to land.

We have to stop looking at what we should fix or change about ourselves and rather look at what is good and learn to embrace it. If you do that, the rest will fall away. The icing on the cake is as you stand your ground, those who love the real you will begin to rise around you. And the approval that you once sought, you will actually get but no longer need. This my friends, is called confidence.

So now I want you too look at the list of things you just wrote down. How can you reframe those idea so that you can embrace them? What part of each concept is the point at which you get... stuck? Begin to consider that your perspective is a little skewed. Write down a *new* version of those statements that feels true. That as you reframe and redefine, you are able to embrace, own and fully stand in.

CHAPTER 5

I AM GOING TO PROPOSE something radical: Your value is not rooted in your ability to DO something for others. It is not about what you GIVE. Your value is innate. As a living breathing being, it cannot be increased or decreased by what you DO.

Imagine you have just adopted a puppy. You get them a few toys, a kennel, some pee pads, and bowls for food and water. You think you've laid out everything necessary to meet their needs; however, by the end of the first week this puppy has chewed through all your shoes, has peed on every carpet in the house, and won't stop toppling his water bowl and making a mess. Now, your first reaction might be that your puppy is just a "bad one." But what if they have a need you aren't meeting? Instead classifying your puppy as "bad" or giving up and bringing them to the pound, you decide to figure out what that need IS and meet it. You take them to doggy daycare to get in their socializing and get all their wiggles out in the process. Therefore, keeping your house in better order AND meeting the puppy's need for socialization and exercise.

The point is, your puppy wasn't "bad." They were displaying some arguably "bad" behavior because their need for socialization wasn't being met. So, the ultimate question is: at their worst, did your puppy's inherent value diminish? Were they worth *LESS* when they were peeing on carpets and chewing your shoes? No! Was their behavior... annoying or inappropriate/disruptive? Yes. But the inherent value of the puppy didn't diminish because of its bad behavior. They were showing you, in the only way a puppy knows how, that they wanted attention. That they had a need that wasn't being met. Did the behavior need to be addressed and changed? Yes. But their need for socialization is still valid and important. Therefore, you find a way to meet the need that is more constructive, but you don't ignore or devalue the puppy or his needs.

Your puppy has value. And their needs have value too.

Okay, so who cares? Why in the hell am I rambling on about this? What does this have to do with people pleasing? Well, (follow the logic) if your puppy and their needs have an inherent value, then surely YOUR needs have inherent value, too. THIS is important. This is what needs to be understood first and foremost. You may think "yeah I know this." But do you? Do you really know this? Are you meeting your body's NEED for rest, when you picked up a shift at work when it wasn't necessary? Okay, so now you are thinking... well, that wasn't a need. That was a desire. I *wanted* to have a lazy day, but I didn't *NEED* it. Well, here's a challenge: what if your desires are your own particular personality's way of meeting your needs? What if you're wanting a lazy day, was actually your body asking you for rest because it needed it? What if rest was the key to you having some peace and joy in your daily life? And if peace and joy are a need, taking a down day is a way of meeting that need?

Some of you are going to have a hard time swallowing this. I know... it seems so *selfish* right? And, of course, selfishness is "bad" so we shouldn't want that (God forbid!)

Well, what if selfishness and self-centeredness are DIFFERENT things?

Think of when you are on an airplane and you are supposed to put your air mask on first, before you put someone else's on. That's technically selfishness. But focusing on yourself, so that you can be your best for the sake of others, is a good thing, right? That's what selfishness is! So, what's the difference between selfishness and self-centeredness? Self-centeredness is seeing

31

ONLY oneself. It's NOT recognizing the inherent and equal value of those around you. It is the thing we are trying to avoid. It is the thought that your needs have GREATER value than that of others. When the puppy was being destructive, he was displaying self-centeredness. He was showing his immaturity. But as a grown dog, when he needs exercise, attention etc., he sits by the front door to let you know that he needs something. That is him being selfish (paying attention to his needs) without being self-centered (not giving two shits about your need to have a urine free carpet). Does that make sense?

Being selfish actually serves a greater purpose. It allows you to be the best you, so that you can be of service to others.

So, if selfish behavior is okay, and possibly necessary for us to be of greater contribution to the world, why are we not embracing it? Because we have been told it is "wrong," "bad," and "shameful."

Well for the sake of your own inner peace, I ask you to open your mind to the possibility of what I am proposing: perhaps, we need to look at things differently. Look at things from a new perspective and challenge what we believe. Because if we continue to do what we've always done, we will continue to get what we have always gotten. Which, let's face it, if you are a people pleaser is: exhaustion, annoyance, frustration, and overall dissatisfaction.

So then, let's propose for the rest of this book that what I am saying is true. That you have inherent value, your needs have inherent value, and perhaps your desires have inherent value (as they are a means to getting your needs met).

Now answer me this: what do you want?

Sometimes there is a misconception that knowing what we want is really easy. I'm guessing you can give me a list of what you DON'T want, but do you know what you DO want? I have struggled with this immensely, and I am guessing you have to. I honestly think this is harder than the "who am I" exercise. The issue we have with the 'what do I want' question stems from the fact that we all have hidden beliefs that help us determine what is ok to want, whether we're allowed to have it, whether it's even possible to achieve. A lot of times, there's disappointment, hurt, failure, shame, or fear around wanting the things that we want. We've either wanted them in the past and it hasn't worked out, or people have told us that we don't get to have that. Or better yet: you get to have this thing you want but only under a particular condition.

Can you relate to this?

The reason that we first want to get clear on who we are is

because we're going to pull on that strength when facing the fears and the false beliefs that shroud what we want. Which is why we are going to do a dream exercise.

I want you to set aside 10 minutes for this exercise. During this time, I want you to dream. Let it be as wild, big and crazy as you can make it. Remember, no one is reading this except for you. So, just let it flow out of you (even if it feels ridiculous or impossible — those are actually the juicy ones!) There are no rules or limitations, this is about allowing what's in the deepest crevices of your heart to have a voice.

As you do this exercise, focus on your feelings. Do you want to feel relaxed, or do you want to feel happy and at ease? Is your desire to just breathe and believe; to let go and have everything just flow to you easily? Think about what it looks like and how those feelings could be interpreted within the context of your daily life. Is your dream a specific career? Is it a set of material things? Does it involve other people? Be as specific or as general as you want. There is no right or wrong dream.

The idea is to dream and to not strategize. No strategizing. This is not a how-do-we-get-there session. Take that off your shoulders. Don't worry about that. This is just dreaming. Give yourself permission to dream about what you want your life to feel like, the things that you really truly want.

GURL Please

Use this time that you have set aside and just dream. If you sense yourself strategizing, if you find yourself asking 'how do I make that happen?' Stop. Just stop what you're doing. Walk away from it, and come back later. No strategizing. That is counterproductive. That will not help you, so don't do it.

Just dream.

_____

_____

_____

_____

_____

_____

_____

_____

_____

_____

_____

Katie Hulbert

_____

_____

_____

_____

CHAPTER 6

HOW DID THAT FEEL? WHEN was the last time you took time out of your life to sit and just dream? Feels kind of exciting, doesn't it? It can also feel super daunting or unattainable, which then feels depressing. Did you feel that too? That deflated feeling? This is where the work starts.

A lot of times what happens is we have those dreams and it triggers an internal reaction as you start thinking about them. The reaction is 'oh yeah, that's not really possible,' or you feel yourself deflate as you think 'that's a freaking pipe dream, so unrealistic, that's never happening for me.'

You will most likely have a lot of things that come up. The reason that we're talking about this is because if you are not fully, and wholeheartedly, going after your dreams there is a REASON for it. It's not because you haven't gotten around to it. It's usually because there is something you are believing about the dream, that is stopping you from pursuing it. The truth is that what you believe determines how you show up in the world and what you receive. Quite frankly, I've never heard of a dream that hasn't already accomplished in some form or fashion by someone else. So, if you aren't going after it, it's not because it's impossible. It's because for some underlying reason — which you are about to uncover — you believe it's impossible *for you*.

Ouch.

Yeah, that one hurt.

There is also another thing that can come up when you do this: fantasy. Sometimes, we don't have dreams; we have fantasies. So, what do I mean? A fantasy is something we concoct in our head, in order to escape our current reality. It is different than a dream. A dream is the fulfillment, and transformation of our reality into its highest form. A fantasy is usually something we create because we don't believe we can have our dream.

Let me give you a real example to demonstrate the difference.

I had a client who I asked to do this exercise. She came back after doing it, head hanging low, feeling awful. I asked "why the long face?" and she began to tell me that her dream *didn't* involve her husband and kids. OOPS! She felt awful about this, because she genuinely loved her family. She didn't truly want to have a life without them. But when she dreamt, she imagined a life on a tropical beach somewhere, solo, drinking cocktails and soaking up the sun. As we worked through this, what became clear was that her actual dream was to have the ease, joy, and peace that this beach fantasy represented. She was convinced that it was impossible for her to have that kind of ease in her current life-circumstance, so her dream (a.k.a. fantasy) just by-passed the issue, instead of finding a way to surmount it. So, the work for her became this: how can I incorporate the need for ease and joy into a dream, rather than a fantasy? What would that look and feel like within my current life-circumstance?

I am going to give you another exercise: I want you to write down all the negative emotions and ideas that are bubbling up inside of you. What thoughts come up when you look at your dreams? The negative ones that make you want to give up. You need to confront all the icky things that are holding you back. Nobody wants to admit that they're believing something really negative about themselves. We all want to be able to say that we believe in ourselves, that we have faith, etc... This is because we've been taught that we have to have this positive mindset all the time. The truth is, we want to get to a positive, hopeful place, but it needs to be grounded in truth otherwise it doesn't work. We need to be able to better understand ourselves and challenge the things holding us back.

Give yourself permission to just feel, think, and say whatever you need to in order to release what's hidden. A lot of times, for myself and for others, it can be a block—this idea that 'well I shouldn't think these things' or 'I shouldn't have doubt.' I shouldn't, shouldn't, shouldn't... As soon as we have a negative feeling, we judge ourselves for having the negative feeling, and then we shut the whole process down. How crazy is that?

Well that only serves to keep the fear and judgement locked in place; if you judge the negative feeling as a "bad" thing, then you feel shame about having the negative feeling in the first place and you shove it away to forget you ever had the negative feeling. This is all because we have been taught that "negative" feelings are bad and shameful (so, we avoid them at all costs). What kind of bullshit is that? Why have we bought into this? Is it the church perpetuating this? The bible says, "Be angry and do not sin," but it doesn't say "don't be angry" it just says: "when you are angry don't be a dick" (Katie's translation). We have to forget this idea that having negative feelings are to be avoided.

Again, they are like poop: what goes in must come out. If they are buried inside, they gunk up the system and create lots of problems internally. And guess what? Beliefs and negative emotions are the same. You can give them a voice, and they will just pass through; or you can stuff them down and poison yourself in the process.

We get so stuck in judging ourselves for not having better faith, or being positive or hopeful. We think 'these are not the doubts I should be having about what's possible for my life.' You want to know what I think of that? Fuck that noise! Tell it to be quiet. You do not get to judge yourself. I am not giving you permission to do that. But I *am* giving you permission to have every negative thought that rears its ugly head. For the purpose of this exercise, let the shit come up. Whatever it is, whatever false belief is rattling around in your head; you have to own it, because you cannot give away what you don't own. What do I mean by that? You can't give someone a plant that belongs to your neighbors, you can only give away what is rightfully yours. If you do not OWN your thoughts, feeling and beliefs... you will not ever really be able to let them go. Eventually we want to analyze whether it's true or not, so that you can let it go. It won't go anywhere if you just keep shoving it away.

You have to give it a voice because it's not going to magically disappear. Whatever is blocking you, is blocking you for a reason. So, give it a voice. And why is it important to give a voice to your subconscious thoughts? Because your subconscious is actually running the show.

Consider this: a three-month-old baby already has a fully functioning subconscious mind. Your sense of logic, however, is not fully developed until the age of 12 or 13. So, for the majority of your childhood, you only have your subconscious mind to help you build a belief and value system that will guide you for the rest of your life. This means that everything you experience as a child is actually shaping the way you see the world and how you react to it. You are relying on your emotions to make snap judgements and draw conclusions about the world and your place in it. And now, as an adult, you are being guided by the belief system you built as a child.

Unfortunately, some beliefs can be created/influenced by trauma or loss. For the purpose of this book, I am not going to address the complexities of that (I do have other resources on that specific topic through my website if you are looking for more in-depth help); however, I will discuss how to uncover the belief system that you have built as a result of that trauma.

As someone who's been through her share of shit, I can tell you this: the biggest change in my life came when I started to understand what I'm sharing with you in this book. The trauma and pain was real and needed my attention. That being said, what I came to believe about the world as a *result* of those traumatic events was actually what needed the most fixing.

GURL Please

I was able to make bigger changes in my life by allowing myself to see the truth of what I was believing (I suck, I'm disgusting, I never get to have love, etc…) than I ever had in all my years of therapy combined. I have learned that it's not always important to understand how the belief got there, but to just see it for what it is. Let the shit come up, and deal with it. It's the only way you can consciously decide if you want to keep believing it.

So, what you're going to do now, is you're going to write down now all of the things that you feel coming up when you think about your dreams. Look at the list of dreams you wrote down. Allow yourself to feel and react to them. What is your reaction when you read them? Set aside at least 10 minutes and start writing it down. Let it flow. Don't edit and don't judge.

As I said, you may have some emotional things attached to it. That's okay. If you need to cry or be angry, or upset... allow it to surface. And for God's sake, don't judge yourself for what comes up. It's okay.

_____

_____

_____

_____

_____

_____

_____

_____

_____

_____

_____

_____

_____

_____

_____

_____

_____

_____

_____

_____

_____

_____

Okay, so you've written down all your limiting beliefs. Now, I want you to look at what you wrote. Sometimes, you will discover you have some crazy stuff under the surface. I recently used this strategy to explore my issues with wealth. What you need to know is that I have always been very frugal, I have no debt and I make enough money to live comfortably (but not extravagantly).

I've attended plenty of workshops around abundance and wealth, and none of them helped me. I knew there was something blocking me, because I would always internally shy away from the idea of "wealth," but I could not figure out why. So, I did this exercise and it hit me like a ton of bricks: I had decided somewhere along the way that if I had any excess money, I had to be responsible with it. I could only spend it if absolutely *necessary*. Or option 2; I had to find the most worthy recipient to whom I could donate the excess. Therefore in my mind, excess money equaled excess responsibility. Well, that concept was so overwhelming to me, that my mind decided that it would rather not have any excess money at all (that way I wouldn't have to figure out what to do with it).

This realization was earth shattering. I had never given myself permission to be frivolous with money in any way. Money in excess was too much of a responsibility, so I didn't want it. Well, as you can imagine, I denounced that belief IMMEDIATELY! It's funny, the day after this happened my car tires blew. And anyone who knows me knows I would normally have tried to find some super deal on used tires, or found a way to not have to buy a whole new set. But, praise the Lord, I walked into the tire store, plunked down my debit card and said: "give me the best you got." That was seriously the most freeing spending spree I've ever had!

I tell you this, because our brains our tricky and wicked smart. The truth can be hard to swallow, so we find sneaky ways around it. Sometimes it's easier to let our subconscious hide things away. So, I want you to look at these negative beliefs that come up and then ask yourself these questions: Is this true? Is this serving me? Do I want to believe this anymore? Is this helpful in any way? How can I reframe this belief so that it actually serves me?

I want you to start analyzing and thinking about what you truly believe. Chew on it. Let it marinate in the back of your mind. Don't try to strong-arm your way through it by forcefully thrusting a new belief on yourself. Instead, look at the belief without judgement or shame. Really sit with it. Ask yourself: is this really true for me? And, if it was true at one point, do I still want to hold onto it? What would it take for me to let this go?

There will be some beliefs that have a really strong hold on you. Some are really hooked in there and you're going to think 'yeah, I don't like that belief, but it's there, and it's going to take more than mind-over-matter to get rid of it.'

I want to encourage you to keep working on them. Just because they are deeply rooted doesn't mean they are permanent. It just means it'll take a little more attention from you to pull them out. A really helpful thing to do is to start asking God, or the Universe, if what you are believing is true. Start asking to see what's false about what you are believing. One of the first times I did this, I had a huge breakthrough: I realized I had been living from the place of what I call an "orphan" mindset.

When it came to relationships, I took whatever scraps I could get. I settled for whatever little morsels were thrown at me (because in my mind it was better than nothing). Now, the hard thing was that this way of being came from years of abuse, neglect and just plain old hardship. And so, it became my way of life. When I did this exercise, I said: "God I do not want to live like this anymore! Show me what's going on and how to fix it."

I'm a visual person, so I receive truth through images. As I sat there and asked God to show me a picture that represented what was happening in my life, one came! I saw this little girl who was wearing a dirty, torn potato sack for a dress. This girl was looking over at this beautiful pink satin dress longingly. I knew this girl was me, and that, although I was wearing rags, I was meant to be wearing that satin dress. As the picture continued to unfold, I saw that my parents had given me this potato sack — not out of hate or disdain for me, but out of their own fear and shame-based beliefs. The message I received was that this was all I was worth. It was all I could ever expect or ask for. And so, I believed it. And I began to settle for whatever I could get. These are the roots I had to pull out. And pull on them I did.

I began the process of retraining my brain to believe that the pink satin dress was my actual destiny. And of course, in my own sassy fashion, this became my affirmation and focus. I kept thinking: 'I get to have that fucking pink dress!'

Sometimes our blocks are just a set of bullshit beliefs that someone threw at us and we accepted as truth. The great thing, and true thing, is that we can stop accepting that "truth" at any time. If you want it to change, seek a truth to replace it. Be open to the truth, revelation, and changes that come. You do not have to force your way into freedom. Instead, you can just allow freedom to be given to you. You only have to choose to receive it. What do I mean receive? It means allowing the unknown to flow into your life, and accepting it. It means letting go of all that's familiar, and opening up to something new. This can feel uncomfortable and sometimes VERY scary; but, being brave enough to choose something different then what you've always known is where change begins. It is the hard part. But it is the best part. The part that will actually set you free :)

Everything you want is up for the taking, the last hurdle is whether or not you can give yourself permission to want what you want. The final key to actually STOP people pleasing is to allow yourself to actually want what you want. Remember in the very beginning I said we want to get to a place of choice? Well, this is where the rubber meets the road: real, true, free choice can only happen when all the options are on the table, to be seen without shame or fear. When choices can be made from a place of total freedom rather than obligation or misplaced loyalty.

When you can give yourself permission to have your needs and desires, and allow yourself to meet them, then you can also choose to lay them down for the sake of another – willingly and freely, from a place of love and choice. You can make a conscious decision; one that is driven by your own power.

You are in control of you. You are no longer being driven by fear, shame, or false beliefs. You are making conscious choices. And, through that new way, you will find peace, congruence and ease as you allow yourself to take charge of your life and decisions. To no longer react to life, but rather to ACT. To no longer be controlled by the needs of others, but rather to be in control of yourself, and act from a place of choice rather than obligation.

- You are of immense value.
- Your needs are of value
- Your desires are of value
- And you get to choose you.

You can then give when from true choice rather than

obligation or fear. There is no honor in sacrifice for the sake of sacrifice. There is only merit when sacrifice is born of love and choice.

And for those of you still thinking who are still unsure, I encourage you to visit my website (www.coachkt.info/spirit) and download the next step of this journey "how to follow the spirit" for FREE :)

EPILOGUE

Okay so I know that there is one thing I have yet to address, that is swirling around in the back of your mind. You are thinking... but what about when people get mad at me? I don't want to make waves, it's just not worth the fall out. So, let me ask you this: what would it feel like to let people be upset with you and still hold your ground? What if it was okay for them to not like your choices, but you still got to make them?

We spend a lot of time and energy trying to convince other people that our decisions are "right" or "good." Why? Because if they validate us, we feel justified. But that means the contrary is true as well: if they don't validate us, we can't validate us either.

So, let me ask you this: what if no one ever had to agree with you or even get your point of view? What if it was okay to not NEED that validation? What if you could be totally cool with the people you love and respect not getting it? Not getting you? What would it feel like to know it's okay that they have a different point of view? For most in this process, this is where the peace actually stems from. Knowing that others can disagree with your opinions without that effecting its validity. That they will still love you, and you will still love them despite the disagreement. It will bring a lot of peace and ease into your life if you can allow for this to happen.

This truth can be difficult to accept, but I'll tell you a story that might help. At the age of 35, I told my family about some sexual abuse that happened in my youth. After I shared this suck-tastic story, I moved out of state for the final time (I had left and come back many times out of my people pleasing misplaced loyalty). During this process, I severed some ties and let go of a few relationships.

These choices were not well received, and I got a lot of push back for my decisions. That was difficult to deal with—it was painful, sad, and I definitely had to grieve the losses that came with my choices. However, I will tell you God's honest truth: my freedom began the day I told my story.

Let me be clear, it did not come from actually speaking about it; rather, it came because I owned it. I owned all of it (the good, the bad, and the horrific). It was my story, and it required my attention and ownership. I began to let go of the need for anyone to believe me, support me, or even understand me. I began to OWN my life. Someone else's opinion no longer dictated how I felt. In my mind, I gave those around me permission to think, feel and believe whatever they wanted. And gave myself permission to do the same.

To this day there are people in my life who don't fully understand my choice. And frankly, that's ok. I no longer need their validation in order to validate myself. In order to be free, you will have to own things that others don't "get," and you will have to be okay with the possibility that they never will. This one is a hard pill to swallow, but it is essential if you want to stand on your own two feet. This is your life, your story. You get to live it. You get to own it. And you get to be okay with others not approving. Contrary to what the world will tell you, you were not created to be "liked." You were created to be FREE. Have you ever been around someone who is totally free? Someone who doesn't care what others think about them? They are totally comfortable in their own skin, and it's infectious!

The "I don't care what others think" attitude isn't callous or hard hearted; it's actually the opposite. It is because of their deep acceptance of self, that they are able to truly love those around them. They love and give from a place of free conscious choice. There is no fear or obligation in the choices they make. They have figured-out that being free to be oneself is not only key to a peaceful life, it's also the key to deep profound love. Because you love freely, give freely, and receive freely.

Your life can be whatever you desire, if you give yourself permission to be the glory and greatness that you already are.

www.ingramcontent.com/pod-product-compliance
Lightning Source LLC
Chambersburg PA
CBHW061158040426
42445CB00013B/1728